Twitter Marketing in 2019 Made (Stupidly) Easy

Vol.1 of the Small Business Marketing Made (Stupidly) Easy Collection

by Michael Clarke

Founder, Punk Rock Marketing

Published in USA by: Punk Rock Marketing

Michael Clarke

© Copyright 2018

ISBN-13: 978-1-970119-10-7

Table of Contents

Chapter 3: 4 Keys to a Kick-Ass Twitter Profile 29

Chapter 4: Yeah, But What the Hell Do I Tweet About? 42

Chapter 5: The Best (and Worst) Times to Tweet 59

About the Author

Michael Clarke is a former cubicle monkey turned social media marketing consultant and author.

He is also the owner of the world's most neurotic Jack Russell Terrier.

Also By Michael Clarke

VIDEO MARKETING IN 2019 MADE
STUPIDLY EASY

FACEBOOK MARKETING IN 2019 MADE
STUPIDLY EASY

PINTEREST MARKETING IN 2019 MADE
STUPIDLY EASY

INSTAGRAM MARKETING IN 2019 MADE
STUPIDLY EASY

LINKEDIN MARKETING IN 2019 MADE
STUPIDLY EASY

EMAIL MARKETING IN 2019 MADE
STUPIDLY EASY

SEARCH ENGINE OPTIMIZATION IN
2019 MADE STUPIDLY EASY

A Special FREE Gift for You!

If you'd like FREE instant access to my seminar "How to Make a Damn Good Living With Social Media (Even If You Hate Social Media" then head over to **PunkRockMarketing.com/Free**. (What else you gonna do? Watch another "Twilight" movie?!)

Prologue: What Am I Gonna Do With 140 Characters, Anyway?

~~140~~ 280 characters. That's what ya get.

That's the character-limit Twitter imposes on its micro-messaging platform.

And even ~~140~~ 280 characters is at the uppermost limit of what people can handle these days. (Tweets 120 characters or longer are seen as "verbose" and get read and engaged with far less than their less "wordy" counterparts.)

Doesn't give us much to work with, does it? (And it doesn't speak well of our "sad, illiterate world" - as my old English lit professor used to call it.)

And yet if we're gonna live in this ADD-inflicted, attention-span challenged, "everyone is a smartphone zombie" apocalypse, then Twitter might be the ultimate weapon in finding new zombies…err…customers who'll buy our products and services.

Because no content platform dispenses information as quickly, efficiently, and effortlessly as Twitter. With a simple scroll on a smartphone, a user can get updates from hundreds, if not thousands, of different sources on the "Twitter roller coaster."

And though Twitter doesn't offer the lasting impact (or at least not at the outset) that platforms such as Facebook or Pinterest do, the fact that human life in the 21st century is only gonna get more hectic, more overwhelming, more disjointed…

…plays into Twitter's greatest strength.

Its ability to let people organize the world in a small, digestible way.

And if you're somehow able to become a trusted

resource in a person's smartphone organization of the world - and in this book I will show you how to do that - then not only can you turn that one follower into a possible customer…

…but with a simple click of the "retweet" button you'll find your message shared (and vetted) to hundreds, if not thousands of possible leads. (Who might also share your message with hundreds, if not thousands, of folks.)

Because that's what them zombies do. They multiply.

So, as we plunge into the deep end of the Twitter pool try not to get too bogged down in the weird jargon - Twitter has got a lot of that - or the slightly deranged rants - Twitter has got plenty of those…

…just remember Twitter is like a haiku, that ancient form of Japanese Zen poetry.

It's short. It's rigidly structured. But if you're able to play within the "rules" of the art form then you can create something powerful. (In just minutes.)

And getting serious marketing benefit - in just a minute - is something any small-business non-zombie can appreciate.

So, if you're ready to begin your quest in this post-apocalyptic marketing wasteland, let's learn the LEAST you need to know about the Twitter social platform.

Chapter 1:

A Beginner's Guide to a Very

Strange Tool

"We shape our tools, and therefore our tools shape us."
-Marshall McLuhan

Don't read this chapter.

Seriously.

If you're already using Twitter regularly and looking for some ninja marketing techniques to move the needle on your business, you can skip this chapter.

(You're busy. Ya got things to do. Like watch all those "Law and Order" reruns.)

But if you're a Twitter newbie -- who doesn't know his tweets from his Twitterati -- then I want to assuage your fears by letting you know: My 79-year-old aunt is on Twitter.

And if she can work this micro-messaging service to devious and nefarious advantage - and this is a woman who hasn't programmed the correct "time" on her DVD player in 12 years - so can you.

The REAL learning curve on Twitter is deciphering what all that ridiculously-named terminology means.

So, here's the briefest of brief overviews to help you get a B.A. in Twitter Studies and prepare you for the rest of our journey:

1. The Tweet

This is the building block of Twitter. These are short messages (280 characters max; used to be 140) a Twitter user sends out via their news feed.

Unless somebody "retweets" your tweet, or finds your tweet in a Twitter search, the only people who "see" your Tweets are your followers. This is why getting followers is crucial.

Tweets can be of almost anything: links to your website, or a video, or a blog post, or simply whatever status update you'd like to share with your Twitter followers. ("Just had lunch with Lady Gaga. #NotImpressed")

You can either send a tweet from your Twitter profile page — type in the status bar and hit "update" — or you can send a tweet from one of the many third-party Twitter dashboard tools available.

We'll go over these in a later chapter.

2. The Retweet

This is the "I scratch your back, please, oh please, will you scratch my back…" part of Twitter. This is where a Twitter user "shares" someone else's tweet with their own followers. (Hoping the favor will be returned at some point.)

"RT @JohnnyDepp Think I'll dress up as Jack Sparrow Scissorhands today!"

You can retweet anybody's tweet — your neighbor, Vladimir Putin, that strange man who talks to himself on the subway — meaning you don't have to follow them and they do not have to follow you to share their tweet with your followers.

The "how" of a retweet is pretty simple: You click the "retweet" button either on your Twitter page or on a third-party tool when viewing the tweet.

When you hit "retweet," it opens the tweet into a new field, with the symbol "RT" preceding your tweet. (This is how you can recognize a retweet from a regular tweet in your Twitter feed.)

The COOL part about retweets is that the person you retweeted is sent a copy of your tweet. (Helpful if you're trying to connect with a real Twitter heavyweight, such as Katy Perry or your moody teenage daughter.)

And you also get to throw in your own editorializing before the original message if space permits. (Editorializing and attitude are major pluses on Twitter.)

If you think that clunky "RT" looks too artificial, you can also use the more subtle "Via" to let people know where you got your Twitter content.

3. The Reply Message

This is where you send a message to someone on Twitter, by simply adding their Twitter handle (user name) with the @ symbol in front of it (Example: "Hey @Madonna, what's with the weird British accent?")

But this reply is not private as all your followers will be sent a copy of your correspondence with the "Material Girl." So, don't give away any national secrets here.

The supercool part of this action is that if the person replies — say @KimKardashian responds to your question about "What exactly is your talent, again?" — then all six million of Kim's followers will see the reply. (And you might pick up 1.7 million new Twitter followers/enemies in the process.)

4. The Direct Message

This is like the "Early Bird Special" of Twitter. This is where you send somebody a PRIVATE message on Twitter. (The trick is, both of you have to be following each other to see the message.)

Sure, it's an option and it's something you CAN use with your more intimate Twitter friends, but most people don't use the DIRECT MESSAGE function.

Ever.

And…I don't really know how to say this politely…but sending a DIRECT MESSAGE is a slightly uncool, old-fashioned — eat dinner at 4:00 p.m. — way of doing things.

Reply messages and retweets are the much better way to go.

One thing people often do is set up an automated system where each "new" follower gets an instant DIRECT MESSAGE thanking them for the follow and asking them to check out whatever crap they're promoting.

Don't do this. Nobody reads this crap. (And they come off as very spammy.)

5. The Hashtag

This might be the most misunderstood — though effective — part of the Twitter ecosystem. This is where Twitter users add the # (pound) sign in their tweets followed by a specific phrase. (Example: #Kony2012; #DarkKnight, #RealHousewivesOfDelaware, etc.)

Just remember to have no spaces in your hashtag. (Writing #Dark Knight, is the same as writing #Dark.)

Because there are so many tweets every nanosecond, hashtags are a quick, easy way for your tweets to be found.

Generally, it's best to jump onto an existing hashtag, if you're hoping to reach a large number of people. (But the key is to find the right #hashtag.)

#SelfPub and #SelfPublishing might appear the

same to us fleshy humans, but in the Twitter world the first is still the hands-down winner in terms of number of tweets.

You CAN create your own hashtag, to promote an upcoming special event, or to build interest and momentum in a cause or movement you're behind.

We'll go over hashtag best practices later, just know they're important. (And that most people royally screw them up.)

6. Twitter Lists

Twitter lists are a simple, but effective, way to organize all the info in your Twitter feed.

You can organize your lists by industry, customers, competitors or teenage miscreants who hope to date your daughter…whatever.

7. Twitter Favorites

This often overlooked feature allows users to "favorite" specific tweets.

And while it feels all warm and fuzzy when somebody "favorites" your own tweet, the real benefit comes from your ability to "favorite" tweets that specifically talk about your business.

It's like having a portable list of testimonials you can use to show how your customers connect with your business. (There are even tools that let you publish this info on your site.)

The Journey Begins...

So, that's about it. The rest you'll pick up as you go. This isn't brain surgery, though it may feel like it, after reading the Twitter feed of somebody like Justin Bieber.

It's just a simple micro-messaging tool…that just so happened to have changed the world. And in the next chapter we'll dive into the basics of HOW to make money from Twitter.

Chapter 1 Key Takeaways:

- **The "tweet" is the basic building block of Twitter.** This is the micro-message, maximum of 140 characters, that followers of your account see when you hit "publish."

- **The "retweet" is a way to share other people's tweets with your followers.** It is pre-populated with the designation "RT", but you can remove this and go for something more elegant, such as "Via."

- **The "reply" message is a way for you to "message" somebody on Twitter without them following you back.** Though, be careful, that "private" message will be shared with your followers.

- **The "DM" or "direct message" is a way to send a private message to somebody who is following you.** It's okay, but a bit old-fashioned. And whatever you do, don't set up automated DM's. (It's spammy.)

- **The "hashtag" is a way to categorize your tweets**. These can be very effective for boosting the discover-ability of your content. And allow you to embrace your inner ironic hipster. #HashtagsAreSo2014.)

- **"Twitter lists" are a way for you to create organized lists of Twitter accounts, independent of your main Twitter feed.** A fantastic way to filter your Twitter feed content and spare you the agony of sifting through all the junk that comes through.

- **"Twitter favorites" are a way to highlight particular tweets that catch your eye.** A great way to collect testimonials for your business.

Chapter 2:

How to Make Money With

Twitter

"Anyone who lives within their means suffers from a lack of imagination."

-Oscar Wilde

Ah, yes. Money.

How DO we make money with all this ~~140~~ 240-character crap?

This is the MOST ASKED question I get from would-be Twitter marketers. (Aside from "Why isn't Jennifer Lawrence responding to my tweets?")

So, before we jump into the trenches of creating

your Twitter account, and outlining your Twitter content strategy for total world domination…

I'd like to dig into how all those "retweets and "followers" and weird apps like TweetDeck and HootSuite and TwikiBoo…

…will help you do the one thing the founders of Twitter still haven't figured out how to do…

Make money.

So glad you asked: there are essentially THREE ways to make money with Twitter:

The Direct Approach to Making Money With Twitter

This is simple, and straightforward: You "tweet" out a link through your Twitter account which asks for some action by the person reading your tweet, which directly relates to income.

This could be:

- A link to a webinar you're running.
- A link to a sales page selling your latest

widget.

- A link to a special event you're hosting.
- A link to a product or service you're an affiliate of.
- A link to a coupon or special offer.
- A link to a website squeeze page where you ask for an email opt-in. (Not sure what this is? We'll get to it later.)

Anything that asks people to go to some location and act (so you can either sell them something or market to them in the future) is a DIRECT APPROACH to Twitter marketing.

And trust me, these DIRECT approaches work. (We'll go over in a later chapter just how to use them for top effectiveness.)

But they're like eating gluten-free, vegan (no eggs harmed in the making of this dessert) brownies. A little goes a long way. (And they certainly don't work with everybody.)

The Indirect Approach to Making Money With Twitter

This is more subtle and doesn't have the ROI (Return on Investment) other forms of marketing do.

But, that doesn't mean it's not powerful. Because this is about:

- Answering questions people have about your area of expertise
- Responding to customer service concerns
- Offering to help people who are having trouble (even if it's dealing with your competitor)
- Sharing cool content (that you didn't create)
- Sharing cool content (that you created but lives on a platform like YouTube, Pinterest, Tumblr, Facebook)
- Providing news and important how-to info that improves people's lives
- Sharing personal (but not too personal)

details about your daily life that reminds folks you are not a robot

I would contend, it's the last one that is key. I know all the "social media guides" tell you not to mix business with the personal.

But a quick TwitPic of your Jack Russell terrier chewing a pillow may do more for your marketing than all the coupons and free offers you can dream up.

And an honest tweet about something your company screwed up, and are working hard to rectify, can go a long way toward people seeing you as a trusted and humane company.

And not just somebody who's out for a quick buck. (Even if you ARE just out for a quick buck.)

The Sneaky, Ninja Approach to Making Money With Twitter

Though I use all three of the approaches I'm outlining here, this last one is probably my favorite. Because it isn't as blatantly promotional as the "direct approach" and it's a little more goal-driven than the "indirect approach" …

…and it just frickin' works so well.

And that is by sending Twitter followers to content that lives on my website - whether it be a video or a photo gallery or a how-to blog post - and then "retarget" all those visitors on platforms such as Facebook and Google.

Now it's beyond the scope of a book on Twitter marketing to go too deep on this but here's how ya do it:

- Throw some Facebook and Google retargeting code onto your website. If you don't know how to do this, hire your neighborhood 13-year-old genius to help you do it.
- Find a couple of your best (and super-helpful) pieces of website content. (Videos and short blog posts work great.)
- Share that content with your followers on Twitter.

- Set up retargeting campaigns to "follow" website visitors on Facebook and Google and display your offer to them whether they ever visit your site again.

The cool thing about this strategy is it's cost-effective.

For just $3-$5 a day you can triple the number of leads you get, by simply tweeting out content.

But it's also a great way to break through your would-be customers initial reluctance to marketed to.

You're leading with stuff that helps them solve a problem and then following up later in a place where they feel most safe...on Facebook and Google.

But all THREE approaches have their place in a successful Twitter marketing campaign. And in the next chapter we'll build the foundation for your Twitter marketing strategy of awesomeness...and Twitter profile that kicks serious marketing ass.

Chapter 2 Key Takeaways:

- **There are three ways to market through Twitter**: DIRECT (sales pages, webinars, email opt-ins, affiliate offers, etc.), INDIRECT (brand building, expert status, pictures of your destructive canine, etc.) and SUPER NINJA (sharing our website content and then "retargeting" visitors)

- **The DIRECT method works well to achieve a specific goal.** But conversion rates tend not to be very high.

- **The INDIRECT works well to boost your brand and give your business some much-needed personality.** But the ROI can be fuzzy.

- **The SUPER NINJA approach is probably the most cost-effective way to increase leads and boost sales through Twitter.** Though it requires you have content on your website that actually helps people. (And doesn't just encourage people to buy your vacuum cleaner.)

Chapter 3:

4 Keys to a Kick-Ass Twitter Profile

"Not doing more than the average is what keeps the average down."

-William Lyon Phelps

We ain't gonna spend a ton of time on this.

Frankly, too many Twitter manuals go on and on about the need for a sleek, compelling background to your Twitter profile, before plunging into the deep waters of the Twitter-verse.

Yeah, that may have been important back in the Mesozoic era (you know, way back in 2010), but today few readers of your Twitter updates will see your tweets on the Twitter platform. Most likely they'll consume them via a Smartphone app or on some Twitter dashboard client like HootSuite or TweetDeck.

But there are FOUR KEYS you need to nail down when creating your profile before we start on your journey to Twitter awesomeness…

…and they will all go a long way toward ensuring your Twitter marketing success going forward. So, let's get started with:

Twitter Profile Key No. 1: Pick a Name That Doesn't Suck

When you create your Twitter account, and verify the email connected to that account, you will be asked to come up with your Twitter name, or handle.

You'll be tempted to use the name of your business or company. And most times this will be entirely appropriate. But there are a couple of reasons you may NOT want to do this:

- **If your company's name is super long** - If somebody retweets one of your tweets, your name will be included in that 140-character limit. So, if you go with a Twitter name of @PetesDenverPoolSupplyInc, that'll gobble up precious Twitter real estate. Go with something shorter instead.

- **You want to use your given name** - If you are the "face" of your brand then this will probably be the way to go. Just add a period between your first and last name. (''michael.clarke'' NOT ''michaelclarke.'')

- **You want to distinguish yourself in a crowded marketplace with some personality** - If I were in crowded, corporate field - such as real estate or accountancy or crime-fighting superheroes - then I'd go for something offbeat like @RealtorBob, @TheTaxKillers or

@CrimeFighterJoe.

- **You want to create separate Twitter handles for different areas of your biz** - If you're a big enough fish in the Twitter pond create separate handles to handle separate duties. (Such as: @MatrixSupport, @ShoeBarnSales, @LindsayLohanParoleOfficer, etc.)

Twitter Profile Key No.2: Pick a Twitter Bio Picture That Doesn't Suck

Now, saying I'm not the most photogenic person is like saying Kanye West is not the most "humble" individual.

But I recognize the importance of a good Twitter profile avatar. (This is the small thumbnail photo that accompanies each of your tweets in a follower's Twitter feed.)

And in my experience, here's what you gotta know about Twitter avatar pictures:

- **The ideal size for your bio photo is 400x400.** This ensures your photo doesn't look Pixelated, or any important photo material is cut off unintentionally.

- **Close ups of faces are always better than far away shots.** Forget that pic of your entire staff in the break room. (Nobody will ever see it.) Instead go with a close-up shot of somebody's face.

- **Unless you are a HUGE brand, go with a person over a logo.** Now if you're McDonald's go with the "golden arches." But for most small businesses putting a human person in the photo will pay off more in the long run.

- **Get a professional photographer to take the shot if you can.** This isn't required, but a pro shutterbug will produce something more vivid and eye-catching than that random pic you've got floating around on your iPhone.

- **Go easy on the heavy-duty Instagram photo filters.** I know that's all the rage on Instagram, but those over-saturated bio pics can look strange in the Twitter feed.

Twitter Profile Key No. 3: Use What Your Mama (and the Twitter Bio) Gave Ya

Now we've ugot the username and pretty bio pictures taken over, it's time to focus on the most valuable real estate on your profile - the Twitter bio.

You'd think people wouldn't read this stuff...

But you'd wrong.

I'm continually shocked how many leads and squeeze page opt-ins I get from this tiny little bit of real estate. (People just want to know more about other people, I guess.)

The key, as with any aspect of social media, is to NOT be boring with your bio and to give people a reason to click over to your website or opt-in page.

Here are five tips to remember when creating bios:

1. **Use real words that real humans use.** NOT "We are an Austin-based accountancy firm who provides structured tax solutions for individuals and businesses alike." Instead: "We're based in Austin. We like to save people money with taxes and stuff. Most of us majored in Math. (God knows why.)"

2. **Put a link in your bio EVEN if it's the same as your website link.** As a Twitter initiate, you're provided two opportunities to add links to your site, in your dedicated website link field and your Twitter bio. By far the MOST important link is the one in your bio. (This will be seen when people mention your tweet or add you to a Twitter list.) But point to two different web locations. (Just make sure the MOST IMPORTANT link is in your bio.)

3. **Use Friendly URLS.** A friendly URL is one that appears like humans created it, not some robot in an evil lair. (For example, you'd want to use http://JimsAutomotive.com/Deal…NOT … JimsAutomotive.com/site-Page4as90.aspf.) If you're not sure how to use "redirection" on your website to create a "friendly" URL, contact your local teenage computer hacker. (He/she can help you out.)

4. **You can CHANGE your bio whenever you want.** You don't have to be married to the bio you come up with when you create your profile. If you have a special deal, offer or product, be sure to change up your bio to reflect the new stuff going on.

5. **You can add #Hashtags here.** In a later chapter we'll go over hashtags and the proper use of these strange little inventions, but right now this is a good place to add

them if there are some common hashtags that are used by your industry. (Such as #CruiseVacations or #DogTraining.) Nobody does this. So doing so will really make you stand out from the competition. (And help you get discovered.)

6. **Offers of FREE and discounted stuff do well in your bio, if done smartly.** You don't want to sound too sales-y in your bio, but something like "For your FREE copy of '10 Biggest Plumbing Mistakes Homeowners Make' eBook, head over to http://PlumbingPhoenix.com" would be appropriate.

7. **You CAN put almost anything in your Twitter bio.** Keywords, links to your Facebook page, your email address, your second grade report card. Whatever you want. Just experiment and see what works for you.

Twitter Profile Key No. 4: Get Your Twitter Profile Registered & Recognized

So, this last step is one many Twitter marketers neglect to do, or even know about. But due to Twitter's rather open-source platform, there are many Twitter directories that archive information about almost every single Twitter account.

And all ya gotta do is create an account, and you'll not only boost the exposure of your Twitter account but also get your website some much-needed Google backlink juice. (Never a bad thing.)

Note: For each of these Twitter directories, replace the "username" with your OWN Twitter username.

Here are the top Twitter directories I recommend you head over to and create an account with:

• Twitter Counter - Another good Twitter directory that lets users get a detailed look into their

Twitter activity over time.

- Twitaholic - Another Twitter monitoring tool. Lets you know where you rank geographically. Not that useful, except as a directory backlink.

- Retweet Rank - Don't worry about where you rank with this tool. It's just another way to get people back to your website.

Chapter 3 Key Takeaways:

- **Choose a Twitter handle that sounds fun, but descriptive.** (Avoid complex, dull-sounding corporate names.) If you're gonna use your real name, be sure to separate your first and last name with a…"period."

- **With Twitter profile photos go with 400x400 square pics.** Also, try to use close-ups of human faces, over impersonal logos.

- **Fill out your bio with key information about your company that doesn't sound like a press release.** (Don't forget to put your most important link in your bio, even if it's the same as your website link.)

- **Change your bio to reflect your latest product or service you're offering.** Links to FREE downloads, reports, videos or offers do really well. Add relevant hashtags to help your profile get discovered.

- **Boost the visibility of your tweets by**

adding your Twitter account to Twitter directories. Some even let you edit your specific bio and add your social links. (All good stuff!)

Chapter 4:

Yeah, But What the Hell Do I Tweet About?

"The secret of getting ahead is getting started."
-Mark Twain

Okay, so you've got a killer Twitter handle picked out and your bio is optimized for marketing/cool person awesomeness.

Meaning you've got some juicy links in your Twitter bio that point back to webpages that can make ya some money.

Must mean you're ready to get out there and grab those 2,500 Twitter followers who'll voraciously devour everything you tweet and send you thousands of dollars a month by buying your stuff!

Eh…not quite.

First, you've got to show a nice mix of Twitter activity on your profile before anybody will even consider following you. (And getting people to follow you is what this whole Twitter marketing thing is all about.)

I would shoot for AT LEAST 20-25 tweets before you even try to get followers en masse. This will make you look less like a spammer, and more like a human being.

Which I hope you are.

So what should those 15 tweets be?

Well, I think they should be as diverse as your regular Twitter activity going forward.

So, now's as good a time as any for me to introduce you to my:

Ultimate Punk Rock Marketing Brain-Dead Tweet Formula

These are the five areas of my Twitter portfolio I stick to religiously. It's a breakdown of how I organize my tweets and schedule them throughout the week, in a variety of markets.

It doesn't matter whether you tweet 20 times a day or just once after lunch, follow this formula and you'll be SURE you're hitting all the important touchstones.

The Formula works like this:

- **20% of your tweets should be helpful, How-to Stuff.** This includes links to interesting blog posts, articles, industry-specific advice, the secret to why people watch the Kardashians, etc.

- **20% of your tweets should be Inspirational.** This includes inspirational quotes, motivating pictures, stories of courage, anything that make us hate the human race a little less. (I know this seem irrelevant. It's not! This stuff will get shared the MOST.)

- **20% of your tweets should be FUN.** These are funny videos, silly jokes, amusing questions, your snarky little comments about whatever, etc. (Bonus points if it has to do with movies, TV shows, or anything entertainment-based.)

- **20% of your tweets should be Retweets of Big Influencers in Your Industry.** Now some of the inspirational and how-to stuff you share CAN be retweets. (And that's okay.) Just be sure to retweet folks you KNOW your customers are following. (If ya get a retweet you might just find a whole new audience waiting to check out your stuff.)

- **20% of your tweets should be Promotional.** This is stuff that directly boosts your bottom line. Such as: links to webinars, contests, opt-in offers, coupons, sales pages. Now I don't recommend this ALL be sales-y stuff. (Doesn't work that well.) Instead, sprinkle in plenty of links to your own video rants…err…how-to content.

The BIGGEST problem most small biz folks make with Twitter is their balance of promo tweets is way too high. Trust me, any over 20% and you'll piss people off.

So what do you do if you want to send more promo stuff to your followers?

Simple…you send out more tweets.

I try to shoot for at least FIVE tweets a day, makes it easier for me to break things up.

One tweet about how-to stuff, one tweet about fun stuff, etc. But you can do more than that. (Many people do.)

Just start out slow and build gradually until you get the feel. In a later chapter, I'll show you some cool automation tools that can make this a lot easier, but for now let me give you a few quicks resources that can help you put all these tweets together.

Tweet Area No. 1: Helpful, How-To Stuff

This could be almost anything:

- A video related to your industry that helps consumers with an issue they're having.
- An online article about some trend in your area of expertise (people just love trends; makes them feel smart).
- A blog post featuring a LIST of the top (whatever) that people absolutely need to know about (the only thing people love more than trends are numbered lists)

And where you find these pieces of kick-ass content will depend on your business, but here are go-to resources I never leave my Twitter home without:

Google Alerts: This is so simple, it's criminal. All you do is set up an alert based on a specific phrase, such as "pool care," and Google will email you the latest news articles, blog posts, and message-board ramblings around that subject. (Be careful, though. The alert will grab EVERYTHING. So, if you put in "pool" you'll get articles about chlorine levels and pool sharks.)

YouTube: There is a video about almost anything. (Don't believe me? Just search for "Japanese poodle fitness video" and you'll see what I mean.) So, do a keyword search for your subject and share all the good helpful stuff you find. Just be sure to pick a video that has a majority of "likes" or "thumbs up." You don't want to share crap. (And there's a metric ton of crap on YouTube.)

AllTop: If you're not familiar with AllTop, then let me introduce you to your new Twitter best friend. This site is basically a blog aggregator (fancy word for collector of good stuff) broken out by subject. Not that extraordinary you say? Yeah, but this site uses humans, not robot algorithms. So, you can bookmark the relevant page for your business and share the best human-endorsed stuff around.

The Big News Sites: I scour Yahoo, New York Times, and CNN every once in a while to see if something interesting is happening. Most of them will even email you the most popular stories. (Hint: If it's popular for them, it'll probably be popular for your followers.)

StumbleUpon: I love this site because it's just so frickin' random. You can find ALMOST anything on StumbleUpon. Photo blogs devoted to locations that look like James Bond villain hideouts. Interior designers imagining what TV show houses REALLY look like. An infographic showing you how to never pay a utility bill ever again. As long as you keep your interests relatively focused, you can find some amazing stuff here.

Tweet Area No. 2: Inspirational

Inspirational quotes do little for me. But I am in the vast Twitter minority.

Of all the kinds of tweets I've sent out over the years — in markets as diverse as self-publishing, real estate and even golf — by far the most retweeted, most shared and most downright "viral" have been quotes.

I think this is because of all the kinds of content floating in the world of social media they are so easily consumed.

You may not have time to read a blog post while you're checking your phone in the bathroom — and don't kid yourself, everybody does this — but who doesn't have time to read a single quote.

And "sharing" a quote can make you look smart. And witty.

And whatever the hell other reason people love quotes.

So, what quotes do you share?

Well, I think this depends on your business.

If you're running a restaurant, you'd want quotes about the joy of eating, drinking and being thoroughly merry. If you're a golf instructor, you'll want to share nuggets about maximizing your potential and not going insane working on your short game.

I think no matter what your business, quotes that underscore some form of: "Life is Short; Appreciate What You Got; Be Your Best" are usually winners.

And where do you find these choice tidbits of wisdom?

Well, you could do a simple search for "quotes" on the good, old Google. But I prefer not to have to work that hard.

So, I simply outsource it.

Two sites I highly recommend are Upwork and Fiverr. These are sites that help you find virtual assistants who, for a small fee, will do things such as collect quotes for your tweets…or even handle all of your Twitter duties.

When I NEED quotes I create a posting and mention I'm looking for a Virtual Assistant to help me collect 200-400 quotes on a SPECIFIC TOPIC. (You gotta be specific!)

This can cost as little as $10-$15. (And it can make a huge difference to your business.)

Tweet Area No. 3: Fun Tweets

This is where a lot of business folks on Twitter really miss out. They forget that social media is SUPPOSED to be social. (Not a platform where you hawk your wares endlessly.)

But sharing funny pictures, silly videos, random and crazy blog posts can be some of the best Twitter content to move the needle on your business. (And some of the most "shared" stuff you put out there in the Twitter-verse.)

Here are my go-to spots for fun Twitter material:

PopUrls: If you're looking for a way to waste time, this site is it. PopUrls aggregates EVERYTHING on the Internet. (Scary, huh?) I find most of my funny, weird gems here.

BuzzFeed: This is like PopUrls, but with a racier edge. (Which CAN be a good thing.) Whether it's the top porn search terms by country or the best soul-dancing videos, the random collection of weirdness that is BuzzFeed has got it all.

The Onion: I'm an unabashed Onion fan. I love their satirical tone and their headlines are hysterical. (Perfect for this Twitter world we live in.) And some of them can be offensive. (Which can surprisingly well.)

Funny or Die: Not everything on Funny or Die, the brainchild of Will Ferrell, is awesome. But most of it is, especially their in-house content. And funny videos do well in the Twitter sphere.

Tweet Area No. 4: Retweets

This one is self-explanatory: You give a little retweet love to a REAL PLAYER in your space on Twitter. (I like to call this "strategic retweeting.") Here are a few tips to ensure your retweets reach maximum effectiveness:

- **Retweet Twitter users whose followers you'd love to get access to.** If they reply or mention you, you'll get an added boost of promotion, and ya might pick up some more followers.

- **Retweet Twitter users who have at least 1,000 followers.** No point in retweeting messages from a ghost town.

- **Retweet stuff that doesn't suck or hasn't been done to death.** Sharing the video of Susan Boyle singing "I Dreamed a Dream" might have been cool three years ago, but it's now second-hand news.

- **Try to put a brief comment before the**

retweet. Example: "You. Must. See. This. RT @jimmy.myers:..." This helps you put your own personality on things and encourages people to follow you. (And not look like some noob jumping on the retweet bandwagon.)

• **Use Twitter lists to find content from just your Twitter heavy-hitters.** We'll go over automation tools in a later chapter, but by creating Twitter lists, and adding high-profile users, it'll make it much easier to find the gold amid all that Twitter crap.

Tweet Area No. 5: Promotional

This is all you! This is stuff that can make you some serious money.

What you promote here will depend on your business model. But here are a few best practices to ensure you get the most Twitter bang for your marketing buck:

- **Sales pages work better if they seem like content.** Saying "Check out the No.1 secret to dealing with hair loss" is better than "Get 50% off the hair loss solution that is sweeping the nation - and will help me pay my bills."

- **Discounts and offers work best for small purchases.** If you're selling something for under $15 or so, then pitch away.

- **Discounts and offers work even better for purchases that have a time constraint.** Limited-time offers and coupons with expirations work like magic. (And people will share them with their friends. Seriously.)

- **Ask for a retweet if space allows.** People generally do what they're told, if they're told by someone they like. (And hopefully the other 80% of your tweets have made you someone they like.)

- **Links to free content that is an upsell in**

disguise work like MAGIC. I love to tweet links to webinars or instructional videos or helpful blog posts…that turn out to be thinly veiled sales pitches. They work well, and they don't make people feel you're a sleazy salesman. (Even if you are.) And you can do that remarketing trick I discussed in Chapter 2.

Chapter 4 Key Takeaways:

- **Divide your tweets equally into FIVE different area**s: 1) How-to 2) Quotes 3) Funny Stuff 4) Retweets 5) Promotional

- **Use YouTube, Google Alerts, AllTop and StumbleUpon** to find the best helpful stuff to tweet.

- **For quotes, either do a Google search** or hire an outsourcer at a site like Upwork or Guru to help you out.

- **For funny stuff,** The Onion, Funny or Die, PopUrls and BuzzFeed are fantastic resources.

- **Set up a list of high-profile Twitter users** and retweet their stuff to get access to their followers.

- **Discounts and coupons work really well** for your promo stuff. (As do free giveaways that opt people into a list.)

Chapter 5:

The Best (and Worst) Times

to Tweet

"The early bird gets the worm, but the second mouse gets the cheese."

-Willie Nelson

This might be the most important chapter you read in this humble tome.

Because knowing WHEN to tweet is almost as important as knowing WHAT to tweet.

As somebody who has listened to all the webinars and read all the crappy blog posts, I know there is virtually NO CONSENSUS about the best time to tweet. (Some will tell you the weekends are best, some will tell you stay away from weekends, etc.)

So, I'll just give you what time periods have worked for me repeatedly. (And I've tested 'em all.)

If you find something in my recommendations that isn't right for you, then tweak where needed.

Note: In a later chapter, I'll show you how to automate all this Twitter activity months in advance.

But in my experience these five principles can help you maximize your ability to market on Twitter, without wasting tons of time sending out tweets that nobody sees. (Or wants to see.)

Twitter Time Principle No. 1: Go Local or Global

What time you tweet will depend on what you're selling. If you're a local business, then your time-zone considerations are relatively tight. (And will probably be during weekday business hours.)

But if you're peddling software solutions around the world, then be flexible with your tweet times.

If you're looking for a hard-fast rule about tweet times, generally anything that hits the east coast of the United States in its Twitter sweet spot (more info in the next principle) is a good rule of thumb.

This is because the vast majority of online eyeballs are in the U.S. eastern seaboard. (East Coasters all believe they live in the center of the world..." and you know what, they might be right.)

Twitter Time Principle No. 2: Working Hours Are Golden

Sorry you night owls, but I find evenings pretty much comatose for Twitter response rates.

Yes, there's less competition in the evenings, but so what? Sometimes there's less competition for a reason.

For me, the absolute best times to tweet are anytime between 9:00 a.m. - 3:00 p.m. EST. So, for me on the West Coast this means I sprinkle my tweet times like this:

- 6:00 a.m. PST
- 7:30 a.m. PST
- 9:00 a.m. PST
- 10:30 a.m. PST
- 12:00 p.m. PST

But this will all depend on what your business is and who you're trying to reach. The big thing is: Don't tweet BEFORE 7:00 a.m. or AFTER 5:00 p.m. (Unless of course you try it and it totally works!)

And before you worry that my recommendations will force you to overtweet…don't worry! Your tweet will get lost in someone's feed so quickly that an hour and a half is plenty of time between tweets.

But five tweets a day may seem daunting at first. So, if you're looking for a minimum amount when you're just staring out, I would do:

- 9:00 a.m. EST
- 12:00 p.m. EST

- 3:00 p.m. EST

This is a decent way to break in and will get you a ton of traction with your followers.

Twitter Time Principle No. 3: Fridays Really Suck (Especially in the Afternoon)

Whatever it is — maybe the fact our working brains make a mental siesta at the end of the week — Friday afternoons just plain suck for Twitter engagement.

I still schedule tweeting on Friday morning, just to keep the old machine cranking, but it's not where I put my primo content, or my heavy-duty promotional stuff. (If you gotta prioritize, skip Fridays.)

Twitter Time Principle No. 4: Mondays are Okay, But Not in the Morning

Ugh. Mondays.

Not only are they rough on your followers who are getting back into the flow of work, but they're also pretty light on Twitter engagement, at least in the morning.

Unless you're trying to tap into that Monday escapist mindset.

Say you're a travel site offering vacation deals. Then Monday would be a fantastic day to tweet about your Acapulco vacation packages. (Especially in cold climates.)

Or if you run a Mexican restaurant touting "Margarita Monday," then you could do a whole bunch of tweets related to curing the cubicle Monday blues.

This will depend on your business, but putting your feet in the information-overloaded shoes of your customer is always a good starting point when trying to come up with your Twitter scheduling strategy.

Twitter Time Principle No. 5: Weekends are Okay, But Mostly on Sundays

I don't know what it is about Saturdays. But I have zero luck getting any headway with my Saturday tweets.

I know you're different. I know you've got the secret sauce to reach people and change the world, but I find most folks are too busy living their lives to be on Twitter.

Now, if you're someone who does a ton of business on Saturdays, like a realtor or a bail bondsman, then you'll want to jump on the Saturday Twitter boat.

But for me, Sunday mornings and Sunday evenings are the best times to schedule your weekend tweets.

And the 5-7 p.m. range on Sunday nights is just golden.

Maybe after a long weekend with the family, the last thing we want to do is talk to humans. (And would rather be on our phone or computer.)

So, I usually schedule some kind of promotion heavily on Sunday nights. (Engagement goes through the roof, and so do my opt-ins and sales.)

Twitter Time Principle No. 6: What the Hell Do I Know?

Again, what I advise may not be right for your business.

The quickest way to find out how utterly full of crap I am would be to test…and test and test.

Try out different times of day. Give Saturday a go. (Even though I know it won't work.) Tweet 47 times a day. Or at 3:00 a.m.

See what excites your audience. (And if you find something different, shoot me an email. I'd love to know what worked for you.)

But once you find your own secret sauce, don't deviate from your plan.

Once the plan is simple, successful, and repeatable, then you've got something you can scale. (And things you can scale can make you some serious money.)

Chapter 5 Key Takeaways:

- **Determine if you need a global or local presence on Twitter**. (If you are global, shoot for the east coast of America during the morning and early afternoon.)

- **Mornings and afternoons are awesome.** (For starters: try to tweet at 6:00 a.m., 9:00 a.m. and 12:00 p.m. of your desired time zone during the week.)

- **Skip Saturday.** But don't forget about Sunday evening, 5-7 pm. (Great engagement and even better profit potential.)

- **Find your own system** with constant tweaking and testing.

Chapter 6:

Art of the Perfect Tweet

"Have no fear of perfection — you'll never reach it."
-Salvador Dali

We've talked a lot about what you should tweet out to your followers (don't worry, I'll soon show you how to get followers) and when the best time to reach those people who will hinge on every word you say.

But you might ask: What's the best way to organize your tweet? Do you really need hashtags? And should you use all ~~140~~ 280 characters? (Interesting note: Since Twitter expanded the maximum character limit people STILL write tweets that are roughly 140 characters.)

So, let's dig into some of the best practices of how your tweets should be constructed:

Perfect Tweet Tip No. 1: Write Tweets That 120-130 Characters

I know you've got ~~140~~ 280 characters to work with. So why am I asking you to stop at 120?

Because you want to give people "room" to retweet you. If they give you some retweet love and you take up all ~~140~~ 280 characters, then they have to do some editing to get your retweet out there.

And as anybody in the business world will tell you, people are inherently lazy and if you ask them to do anything that takes more than a .001% effort they won't do it.

So keep those tweets short and enjoy the retweet awesomeness.

Perfect Tweet Tip No. 2: Write Tweets Shorter Than 100 Characters If You Can

This one shocked me. But according to Buddy Media, tweets less than 100 characters experience a 17% boost in engagement. (I'm not sure how they define "engagement," but I'm sure it's better than "non-engagement.")

So, if it's possible, keep your tweets nice and short. (It'll make your tweets stand out from the usual crap.)

Perfect Tweet Tip No. 3: Place Your Link About 25% of the Way Into the Tweet

According to social media savant Dan Zarrella over at HubSpot the highest engagement on Twitter comes from tweets with links approximately a quarter of the way into the tweet.

So…

"Apocalypse is near: http://bitly.463 Michael Bay to remake Mutant Ninja Turtles"

…is better than:

"Apocalypse is near. Michael Bay to remake Mutant Ninja Turtles: http://bitly.463"

I have no idea why. I don't care. It's worked for me, and it'll work for you.

Perfect Tweet Tip No. 4: Kill the Passive Voice and Use Active Verbs

Twitter is like poetry. Ya gotta be tight and economical with your words. So, this wouldn't be super awesome:

"We are presenting a webinar later this afternoon, where we will discuss the merits of Twitter marketing http://bit.ly/twitter"

But this would be a helluva lot better:

"Crush your competition with Twitter. Find out how in this kick-ass webinar TODAY:

http://bit.ly/Twitter"

Did ya notice how all those active verbs gave some urgency to the copy. That's what they do! (Let them do most of the Twitter heavy lifting for you.)

Perfect Tweet Tip No. 5: Don't Forget About Hashtags

Have to be honest. For the longest time I never used hashtags. (Just didn't understand their appeal.)

Well, was I a total moron. People love 'em and they can help your tweets get discovered.

There are three basic ways to use hashtags:

1. **Group your tweets within an existing hashtag category,** such as #asklochte; #writerquotes; #thingsgirlsdo; #tweetevent. The best place to find this info is at Hashtags.org and leverage the work somebody else has already done to find the optimal hashtag. (Don't reinvent the wheel - just steal it!)

2. **Create your own hashtag to brand your event, company or special offer.** This is a powerful strategy, and one that can get people to do a lot of social promotion for ya. Just be sure to research your hashtag before using. (The dessert company Entenmann's got in trouble for using the hashtag #notguilty at the same time supporters of murder suspect Casey Anthony were also using #notguilty. Uh, awkward.)

3. **Use a hashtag ironically,** such as #NoMoreShaveTech or #WhatWouldMichaelBayDo. This one may not have an immediate marketing benefit, but it can make you seem funny, articulate and somewhat human. (Even if you aren't any of those things.)

Perfect Tweet Tip No. 6: Try to Use a Real Hyperlink (If Possible)

If you're using any kind of automated Twitter service, such as TweetDeck or HootSuite, they'll usually offer some form of link shortening service.

Don't do it. (If you can.)

Putting a "real" hyperlink — http:yoursite.com/coupon as opposed to http://bit.ly/78$#2 — will boost your click-thru rates and help put some moolah in your pocket.

One exception to this might be the Amazon affiliate program, which lets you create an Amazon shortened link that looks something like "http://amzn.to/1lqbBXY." Here, you are leveraging the power of a big brand like Amazon.)

But I haven't done enough testing with this to determine its effectiveness. Stay tuned on this one!

Perfect Tweet Tip No. 7: Use Interesting Characters to Let Your Text Stand Out

Anything that helps your tweets stand out is a good thing. And I mean anything.

I love the tilde… (~)

It's just so weird and can convey, well, whatever the hell I want it to convey.

Colons (:) are also good right before a hyperlink.

As are any variety of characters: ($, %, ^, *, &)

And even ALL CAPS can be effective. (Just don't go overboard.)

And if you are going to feature a blog, video, or picture then be sure to add the following before the tweet:

- [BLOG]
- [VIDEO]
- [PIC]

It will help boost click-thru rates. (And make

your tweets stand out in an overcrowded twitter stream.)

Chapter 6 Key Takeaways:

- **Keep your tweets between 120-130 characters** to allow easy retweet-ability. (Don't make people THINK to help you.)

- **Keep your tweets below 100 characters** for maximum engagement.

- **Put your link a quarter of the way** into your tweet.

- **Get to the point.** Use verbs. Skip adverbs.

- **Use hashtags** to promote your special event or brand. (Be sure to check nobody is using the tag.)

- **Use real links** (if you can.)

- **Use interesting characters** to make your tweets stand out.

Chapter 7:

How to Get a Million

Followers in 24 Hours

"To handle yourself, use your head; to handle others, use your heart."

-Eleanor Roosevelt

Okay, so maybe a MILLION followers are optimistic. But 500K for sure. :)

Seriously, though, we have come to the most CRUCIAL yet MISUNDERSTOOD part of Twitter marketing.

And that is: How to get some frickin' followers who can eventually turn into customers who put money in your pocket.

I must warn you though; this section is not for the timid.

If you don't like to offend or step on toes, then the techniques outlined here may not be for you.

But if you want to get a ton of Twitter followers quickly (but not so fast as to raise any red flags with the Twitter gods), then these tips will be right up your Twitter marketing alley.

So, here are my THREE Totally Ninja Techniques for Getting a Crapload of Twitter Followers Fast:

Ninja Technique No. 1: Follow to Be Followed

I know what most of the gurus tell you.

Mass following people on Twitter is spammy. And it's unethical. And it makes you look like a huckster.

Yeah, but it works. (If you do it right.)

The key is to have a plan and work that plan. (Without all those crappy mass-follow automated solutions that seem to spring up every week.)

So, here's what I do with every new Twitter account I've created, and it has worked EVERY single time.

1. **Find your tribe.** Choose 15-20 "big-time" Twitter users (at least 2K followers) whose followers represent your ideal customer. (Could be a competitor, a local celebrity, your favorite chef, the President of Denmark, etc.)

2. **Schedule three "following" sessions a week.** My ideal following times are Tuesday 12 p.m., Thursday 12 p.m., and Sunday 5 p.m. But you can do it whenever you like. (Just avoid Saturdays and late evenings.)

3. **For each session, follow the most recently active followers of 3-5 users on your big-time user list.** This is easy to do. Just find the Twitter profile page of the big-

time user, click on the followers link and follow away. (I usually try to shoot for about 50-100 folks here.)

4. **Try NOT to follow companies or people without profile pictures and written bios.** Unless you're on the B2B (business-to-business) train, you're not interested in other businesses. And people without pictures aren't frequent users. (And folks without bios are usually Russian hackers.)

5. **Give people you just followed TWO FULL DAYS to follow you back and then unfollow any folks who didn't follow you back.** About 40% of everybody I follow will follow me back. (Not always, but it's a good general rule.) It's vital you give people a full two days, otherwise you'll be seen as a spammer and Twitter can shut down your account faster than a Taylor Swift romance.

6. **Go slow.** Twitter has a limit of how many

people you can follow. The maximum number of users you can follow is approximately 10% more than the number of people who follow you. (Example if you got 1,000 followers, then you can follow 1,100 peeps.) But don't worry, stick with it and you'll build a decent following in no time.

7. **Rinse and repeat.**

Ninja Technique No. 2: Put Twitter Buttons Everywhere

The first technique, by far, is the one where I see the quickest gains.

But it's this second technique, in which you place a "follow me on Twitter icon" in specific areas of your Internet footprint, that I see the most lasting and permanent connections on Twitter.

That's because these are people who already have affinity with me and want to know what else

I'm up to.

And people like that make for great Twitter marketing buddies.

The HOW is pretty simple: just head over to the Twitter Button Resource page (PunkRockMarketing.com/TweetButton) to grab some code and make your own icon.

It's the WHERE that so many people neglect. So, here are my favorite (yet often overlooked) places to put a Twitter icon to boost my follower count:

- **Email.** Total no-brainer here, but I'm surprised how many people don't take advantage of the real estate at the bottom of their email newsletters or info blasts that encourage people to follow them on Twitter.

- **Your website.** Here's another lost opportunity for many marketers. Online marketing newbies sure know how to cram a bunch of crap on their website, except for the stuff that actually lets them continue to market to their customers. So throw a twitter icon on your site so the conversation, and the selling, never ends.

- **Blog posts and articles.** If you do any kind of written website content, it's crucial you have some kind of "follow what I'm doin' on Twitter" nearby. (Especially if you're guest posting.)

- **Video.** If you have any kind of video or YouTube presence (and you damn well should), then putting your Twitter info can be invaluable here. (And you will usually get some easy retweets along the way.)

- **Flyers/Print Marketing.** If you have any kind of direct marketing, be sure to include your Twitter handle. Give people a reason to follow, such as: "Follow us on Twitter to find out about our specials." Not: "Follow us on

Twitter to boost my pathetically low self-esteem."

- **Your Front Counter.** If you're a brick-and-mortar business, you're absolutely brain dead if you don't have some kind of thing at the front counter encouraging people to follow you on Twitter. Again, you gotta give 'em an incentive. Free, cheap stuff is usually good.

- **Your body.** I have a client who puts his Twitter handle, along with an offer of a free coupon, on his company-issued sandwich shop t-shirt. Twitter followers went up 300%! (Mostly from people standing in line to buy sandwiches.)

Ninja Technique No. 3: Answer People's Questions

Don't think I'm breaking any news here when I say good business is about helping people solve problems.

But for some businesses this can be difficult. It's hard to find people BEFORE they come looking for you. (Such as a personal injury lawyer or a Justin Bieber life coach.)

But Twitter is perfect for jumping right into the confused and muddled vortex your prospective customers find themselves in and deliver kick-ass solutions.

And all without chasing a single ambulance.

So how do you find people who need your help?

Here are a few super-secret ninja tricks I advise all my clients to use:

- Go to Twitter advanced search.
- Add your industry-specific keywords. In the "All of These Words" field put in your keyword (such as "sandwich" or "pool cleaner" or "dry cleaner") and a "?" (No quotes)

- Strip out the spammers. In the "None of These Words" field, put in the phrase "http" (no quotes). That will remove all the auto-posters (robots).

- Add question words. In the "Any of These Words" field put in "recommend," "how," "find" ...or whatever words you think might fit your particular field. (No quotes)

- If you're a local business, specify your area. In the "Places" field put in your town or city.

- Hit Search.

- Look for questions you can answer. Be cool. Don't be sales-y. Just answer questions like a human being.

Trust me, do this for a little while and you'll be shocked how quickly you can grow a dedicated following. (That just so happens to give you money.)

Social media expert Gary Vaynerchuk built an entire wine-making empire, not to mention an insanely lucrative public-speaking career, by simply answering people's questions about vino.

You can do worse than follow his lead. (Just don't root for his beloved New York Jets. That simply doesn't have the ROI any good business person is looking for.)

Chapter 7 Key Takeaways:

- **Follow the followers of big-time users** in your industry to build up your Twitter following.

- **Be sure to give people you recently followed at least two days** to follow you back. Shoot for three following sessions a week.

- **Put your Follow Me on Twitter icons everywhere** (including email signatures, newsletters, store counters, your employees, etc.)

- **Answer questions** (with the Twitter question search above) to help people out and add people to your Twitter following.

Chapter 8:

Contests, TweetChats & Live Streams...Oh My!

"If you're not gonna go all the way, why go at all?"
-Joe Namath

So, at this point, you pretty much have a master's degree in Twitter Studies.

I think it's safe to say with the knowledge you've consumed so far, you know more than nearly 85% of all business peeps when it comes to Twitter marketing.

But now it's time to take your knowledge to the next level. It's time to get a full-on Ph.D. in

Twitternomics. (Without all the crippling student loan debt.)

Because no matter how many followers, retweets or "engagement" you have, it really doesn't mean a damn thing until you can translate all that Twitter activity into paying customers.

And there may be no better form of social media marketing than Twitter for instantly converting browsers into buyers. Here are a couple of profit-generatin' techniques that work really well:

Super Ninja Twitter Technique No. 1: Twitter Contests

Want to build your Twitter following and customer base fast? Throw a Twitter contest.

People love to win free stuff. And the stuff doesn't even have to be that amazing. I'm constantly amazed at the FREE crap people scurry around trying to win on Twitter. (Imagine what would happen if you actually gave away something decent.)

Here's how to organize your very own Twitter contest of epic proportions:

1. **Come up with a prize that doesn't suck.** Could be an iPod. A dinner for two at your restaurant. A free one-hour consultation in your office. A date with Brad Pitt. Whatever.

2. **Create a special website landing page with details about the contest.** This could be on your blog, your website, your Facebook page, wherever. Just so long as it's a link. Have a picture of the prize that doesn't suck. (If you want a super easy tool for running a contest, give WishPond a try. They've got a FREE Trial that makes the whole process seamless.)

3. **Shorten that special website landing page URL.** This is where you take a clunky, long URL and shorten it using a site like Bit.ly or TinyUrl. (Example: http://bit.ly/89do) This is especially handy if you've got a bunch of extra analytics code

at the end of your URL.

4. **On your contest detail web page, let people know how they can win the special something you're giving way.** You want them to follow you on Twitter and tweet out a phrase of your choosing to enter. (Example: "Just entered to win a FREE iPod. Follow @punkmarketing and retweet http://bit.ly/8&*2 #Freepunkstuff.) The unique hashtag is key. This will let you track entrants into the contest. Don't forget to come up with an original #hashtag nobody else is using. (Sorry but #freestuff is already taken.)

5. **Promote the contest everywhere.** On Twitter, Facebook, YouTube, forearm tattoo, etc.

6. **Allow the contest to run for about 4-7 days.** This will depend on your audience, but I generally like to keep my contests within that timeframe. (Anything longer

feels more drawn-out than a "Downton Abbey" episode.)

7. **Pick a winner.** Use the hashtag search in Twitter search or Bing Social search to find a list of all the people who retweeted your tweet.

8. **Announce the winner...everywhere.** Again on Twitter, Facebook, YouTube, etc.

9. **Wait 6 months and do it again.**

Super Ninja Twitter Technique No. 2: Twitter Q&A

The one problem with Twitter contests is you get a lot of freebie-seekers. (And slightly deranged people should be on meds.)

Which is okay. To a point. But ideally you'd like people who'll give you hard currency for your efforts.

And that's why I like Twitter Q&A's.

The leads I've gotten from Twitter Chats are

much higher than from Twitter contests. (Even if overall numbers are lower.)

And by riffing on your area of expertise, you not only can put a face to your business, but you become the go-to person — in your follower's mind — for your given industry.

Trust me: it's like holding your very own 30-minute infomercial, without all the bad lighting and ultra-expensive ad buys.

So, here's how you run a Twitter Q&A:

1. **Pick a hashtag.** This is important. You'll be using this to not only promote the event but also keep track of who's attending. Make it unique and make it somewhat not sucky. (#AskJim or #AskCompanyName would be good ways to go.)

2. **Schedule a time for the chat.** I think the sweet spot is anywhere from 30-45 minutes, though I've seen people go as long as 90 minutes. (Not something my ADD can handle, but if you can do it, knock yourself

out.)

3. **Promote the event with the hashtag.** This is key. You gotta get the word out about your event. So, make sure everything you've got — your website, blog, Facebook page, Twitter account, back of your car — has the hashtag and the topic you plan to talk about.

4. **Tweet about it constantly.** This is a no-brainer, but still, many small-biz types miss out on this. You gotta let people know what you're doing. (Don't forget the #hashtag.)

5. **Write a press release.** If you think your chat isn't important enough to do a press release, then you should see the crap people write press releases about. Believe me, if you're answering questions in your knowledge wheelhouse, it's worth a press release. (And you can really get the word out. Not to mention help your Google rankings.)

6. **Do the Chat.** Here's how it works. When

the event starts, send out a tweet letting people know to ask questions using the designated hashtag, then retweet their question, so people see it. And then you answer with another tweet. Su-per simple.

7. **Wrap up the chat with a call to action.** Thank everybody for attending and let them know if they've got more questions, or they want to get a copy of whatever free thing you're peddling, then they can reach you at your website. (Be ready to have some way to collect their info. Because they are now hot leads.)

Here's the thing, no matter what business you're in, you have some level of expertise that civilians/possible customers might find interesting.

Ninja Technique No. 3: Twitter Live Video (Via Periscope)

I know what you're saying. Streaming video? On

Twitter? I'd rather watch all 12 "Transformers" movies. (In Bulgarian.)

That's what I thought. Until I did it. And now, I'm only sad I didn't do it earlier.

Whether you're recording a live event or talking from the comfort of your double-wide trailer, live video on Twitter can do some amazing things for your marketing.

And since Twitter purchased Periscope, for an insane amount of money, it now offers the super-simple Twitter Live Video feature.

It is built into the Twitter app — available for either Android or Apple devices — but once you've got installed, you:

- Log in to your Twitter app on your device
- Set up your phone/tablet for recording (Best if you use external microphone and tripod)
- Tap the compose icon (Looks like a pen and quill)

- Tap the live video icon (Looks like..well…a pizza with one slice missing)
- Swipe down and tap "End broadcast" when you're done

And if the thought of broadcasting live video strikes you with mortal fear — it might — you can tap the microphone icon and choose audio-only. (Not sure how interesting that would be, but worth a go.)

I've had clients as diverse as surf-school instructors, caterers and even dentists do these from a variety of locations.

And again something about video makes people "trust" you. (Even when you shouldn't be trusted.)

Chapter 8 Key Takeaways:

- **Throw a Twitter contest** by asking entrants to retweet a designated message. Be sure to use a special #hashtag to track results.

- **Plan a Twitter Q&A** where you can answer questions from folks. Don't forget to send out a press release to promote the event.

- **Do a high-tech Q&A** with Twitter Live Video. Use the Twitter app, along with a tripod and external mic, to get some high-quality live Twitter video out there.

Chapter 9:

The Strange (and Sometimes) Profitable) World of Twitter Ads

"Many a small thing has been made large by the power of advertising."

-Mark Twain

I had no intention of writing this chapter on Twitter advertising.

For three reasons:

- The Twitter advertising platform is so frickin' NEW any proclamations I make

will be rendered obsolete in about a
week

- Though Twitter ads offer great
  targeting, they can royally suck with
  click-thru-rates (Twitter users don't like
  to click on…well…nearly anything)
- If you think CTRs are low with Twitter,
  just take a gander at conversion rates
  when trying to "sell" (Good frickin'
  luck!)

And yet you see before you a chapter on Twitter
advertising: what gives?

Well, though Twitter is not the social media ad
juggernaut Facebook is — no one is — there are still
a ton of great opportunities to be found with Twitter
ads.

Especially if you're not overly "selling."

That's because:

- Hardly anybody uses the Twitter ad
  platform

- If they do use it, they probably suck at it
- If retargeting or lead-capture is your goal — instead of an instant sale — Twitter ads can really pay off.

As my brother-in-law likes to say, "Right bait for the right fish." So, if your customers/fish spend a significant amount of time, Twitter ads can be an effective (and quick) way to boost your bottom-line.

Twitter Ad Strategy #1: Pick a Goal (That Doesn't Suck)

There are five different conversions you can focus your Twitter ad campaigns around:

- New followers
- Website clicks or conversions
- Promoted video views (I like this one a lot)
- In-stream video views (pre-roll)
- Tweet engagements

- Awareness (Whatever that means)
- App installs/re-engagements

I'm not an app/tech guy so I won't "pretend" to advise you on what to do with app installs. (For the longest time I thought "Pokemon Go" was a card game.)

And I don't advise marketers spend a lot of time growing their follower count. (Followers just ain't worth spending much on.)

But my three favorite Twitter ad conversions, in order, are:

1. **Website clicks/conversions** (Great for promoting content on your website)
2. **Promoted video views**
3. **Tweet engagements** (Good for boosting the overall popularity of your Twitter account)

I like to have a healthy mix of all three with my Twitter ad campaigns. My ratio looks something like this:

- 50% of my ad budget goes toward "website clicks"
- 25% of my ad budget goes toward "promoted video views"
- 25% of my ad budget goes toward "engagements"

But this will depend entirely on your business model. If you don't produce a lot of original content, or you've got high-ticket items in your funnel that pay off big, then conversions and Twitter cards are the way to go. But if you've got a content-rich website or you interact with people on Twitter a lot, then "engagements" and "website clicks" will do well for you.

If you've got your website and funnel dialed in. Speaking of...

Twitter Ad Strategy #2: Get Ready for All That Twitter Ad Traffic

Before you spend a penny on Twitter ads you

want to make sure your website, landing pages (and/or sales pages) are "ready" for those millions of new visitors you're gonna get. (Okay, maybe not millions, but you get the idea.)

And by "ready," we mean you gotta:

- Install retargeting code on all relevant pages (This lets you track folks, even if they leave your website without opting in)

- Place "relevant" sidebar and/or footer offers in your content (Don't pitch stuff a Twitter user would never buy)

- Create a Twitter-only landing page to capture opt-ins (Not only keeps analytics organized, but lets you tailor your copy to a Twitter audience)

It's beyond this humble tome to go too deep into the "retargeting" rabbit hole. But here's the Cliffs Notes version of how it works:

1. **Sign up for a Google Adwords and**

Facebook ad account. (You probably already have one of each.)

2. **Grab the retargeting code for both and install on every page of your website.** (If this freaks you out, get a coder at Fiverr do it for you.)

3. **Tell Google and Facebook** which web page represents a successful conversion goal — such as a "Email Opt-In Thank You Page" or "Thank You for Buying" page — for your funnel.

4. **Create ads for visitors who visit your website** — but DON'T reach your conversion page — and encourage them to join your funnel of awesomeness.

This is how I make most of my money with Twitter ads: I send 'em to a content page on my website, and then whether they opt-in or not I continue to market to them.

Sneaky, but effective.

But even if you don't have a ton of content,

you'll be promoting with Twitter ads, you want to make sure you have the chance to "sell" to website visitors again and again and again.

Twitter Ad Strategy Ad No. 3: Pull the Trigger

Because Twitter ads are relatively new — and so few people are having real success with them — I can't tell you definitively the ONE way to create Twitter ads.

But let me share with you the step-by-step methods I use for my Twitter ads. (And if you find a system that works better drop me a line and tell me what an idiot I am.)

Promoted Tweets (and Website Clicks)

Purpose: Great for promoting a contest, live event, or sending people to a web page. (Offers and coupons work great!)

Anything where you want people to leave the

confines of Twitter and take a specific action.

How I Do It

1. **Campaign** - Sign in to Twitter, click on Twitter ads, and name your campaign.

2. **Targeting** - Target either through keywords or similar followers to specific Twitter accounts whose followers represent your ideal customer. I prefer the latter, but test to see which works best for you. (Don't target your own followers!)

3. **Device** - Start with desktop ad placement, then slowly build out to mobile. (And I mean "slowly.")

4. **Tweets** - Manually select 2-4 tweets (or create 'em on-the-spot.) Make the copy clear, informal and personal. Conversational and fun is best. (Example: "Good organic pizza just got easier. Learn how to save 25% off your next Denverlicious pizza pie: link.com" Be sure to use your own analytics

link — Twitter analytics suck!)

5. **Budget** - Set a total budget of $100, and a daily max budget of $10. (Don't worry, you can always pause the campaign if you need to)

6. **Location** - Start with the U.S. and then spread out from there. (Unless your customer base lives outside the good, old USA.)

7. **Pacing** - Pace the campaign evenly throughout the day. (Though if your offer is time-sensitive, then choose accelerated.)

8. **Cost** - Choose a cost-per-click that is 25% of the lowest suggested bid. This ain't Google Adwords where you gotta out-bid everybody else. Keep that bid low — and keep lowering it — until you find a dead spot. (That's your golden range.)

Twitter Promoted Video Views

Purpose: Great boosting the engagement of a

video.

How I Do It

1. **Add the Twitter remarketing pixel to your website, if you haven't already.** Have a designer on Fiverr do if for you if this seems complicated.

2. **Create the perfect video.** I don't mean perfect in terms of quality, but perfect in terms that it's short, interesting and contains a CTA — usually in the text of the ad. This CTA will encourage people to go SOMEWHERE and do SOMETHING after they watch the video. Otherwise it's a waste of money.

3. **Create ad and upload video** - Few people know you can upload your video direct to Twitter without creating a "sponsored tweet." This is why I like this ad. Cuts out any obstacles to a viewer watching the video.

4. **Use the same settings as the Promoted Tweet** - Device: Desktop; Total budget: $100; Daily max budget: $10; Location: U.S. at first, then spread out; Pace: evenly through the day; Cost per click: 25% of lowest suggested bid.

5. **Target your tribe** - Because you get charged for each video view — or Cost-Per-View (CPV) — I like to target people already "following" me on Twitter and folks who've landed on my website. (Leads to better conversions.)

Twitter Ad Strategy Ad No. 4: Find the Winners (Ditch the Losers)

Once you've got a Twitter campaign or two running, it's just finding the ones that work and killing the campaigns that don't.

But how do you know if a campaign is a winner? Well, this will depend on your business. But any

Twitter ad that produces a lead at a cost-per-lead that works for your business model is a winner.

If you're selling $450k yachts, your cost-per-lead will be radically different than if you're selling a $7 eBook.

But here are a couple general guidelines to keep in mind:

- **When targeting @usernames, break your campaigns up in groups of five.** This will help you hone in on Twitter accounts that actually provide the biggest source of your leads.

- **If you're not getting a good response, try running ads between 6pm - 9pm.** (Might just be your audience ain't on Twitter during the day.)

- **Use existing customer demographic information in your Twitter ads.** (If your audience is 65% women interested in the "Food Network" use that intel to further refine your targeting.)

- **When you've got your Twitter ads rocking-and-rolling, try buying a couple of "paid tweets"** — in which you pay folks to spread your message for you. Tools for this include: SponsoredTweets.com, PaidperTweet.com, and BuySellAds.com.

- **Always trust YOUR data, over anybody else's.** Including mine, or Twitter's.

Twitter ads are NOT an overnight strategy. (Not even sure it's an over-fortnight strategy.) But if you've got a compelling offer — or irresistible coupon — the Twitter-verse would be brain-dead to not jump on, then dedicate some time and energy to Twitter advertising.

It may not pay off immediately, and it will take some work, but once you've got it honed in, it can be a surprisingly profitable way to make money, and outpace the competition. (Especially if that competition thinks "Pokémon Go" is a card game.)

Chapter 9 Key Takeaways:

- **Effective Twitter ads start with good goals that don't suck.** The author prefers "website clicks," "video views," and "sponsored tweets." (Skip "followers" — it just ain't worth it.)

- **Make sure your funnel is ready for that Twitter ad traffic before running your first campaign.** This includes setting up relevant offers and ensuring you've got all that retargeting goodness ready for prime time.

- **Set up your initial Twitter ad campaigns following the recommendations above.** (Don't forget to keep your cost-per-click low, and your copy simple and conversational.)

- **Always look to improve your winning ads and ditch the crappy**

campaigns. Try running ads in the evening, purchasing a couple of paid tweets, creating different kinds of Twitter video ads, and using your existing customer demographic information to make sound Twitter ad decisions.

Chapter 10:

Setting It All on AutoPilot

"The first problem for us all, is not to learn, but to unlearn."

-Gloria Steinem

The beauty, and I mean the absolute beauty, of Twitter is that like those cheesy rotisserie grill infomercials…

You can "set it and forget it."

It's possible, if you've got enough content and quotes and funny videos and promotional links stored up, that you can schedule your Twitter activity months, if not years, in advance.

This is because (unlike other social platforms like

Facebook, Pinterest and Instagram) Twitter has what techie types call an "open API."

Which is a nerd-alert way of saying Twitter lets developer-types grab their data and create toys that make your Twitter life easier.

Now, not all third-party Twitter tools are created equal. (In fact, some tool's names are as dumb as the tools themselves.)

There are a few I can't live without. While most of them have a free version, their premium versions can often make your life much easier.

But when you're first starting out, just grab the FREE tools and give 'em a test drive.

Twitter AutoPilot Tool No. 1: HootSuite

I believe the official term for HootSuite is that it's a dashboard client for Twitter.

It's just a kick-ass way to use Twitter and is pretty much my absolute number one tool I use day in and day out.

Why?

Well, HootSuite lets you feed multiple Twitter streams into one single dashboard.

Meaning, if you've got multiple Twitter accounts, you can handle all the scheduling, commenting, retweeting, replying, and cavorting in one place.

But, wait! That's not all! (Cue the music.)

These streams can be virtually anything: LinkedIn profiles and company pages, Twitter searches, Twitter lists, Facebook pages, Instagram profiles, YouTube channels, Pinterest profiles...

So, you can handle all your social media goodness in one place.

The FREE version lets you sync up to five twitter accounts, which is perfect for most businesses. The PRO version lets you handle up to 50 different accounts.

You also get a fair amount of analytics, so you can track what works and what doesn't.

Alternatives include: TweetDeck, SocialOomph and a bunch of other crappy tools I can't stand. For my vote, HootSuite is still the best.

Twitter AutoPilot Tool No. 2: Friend or Follow

The manual labor of having to "unfollow" masses of people in my quest to build up a Twitter follower base can be cumbersome.

But with Friend or Follow it's a breeze.

All you do is:

- Sign up
- Import your Twitter account
- Let the tool show you who is not following you back
- And then "unfollow" everybody who does not deem you worthy of their attention

Now, the process isn't as automatic as it once

was. (Afraid you'll have to THANK Twitter for that. They changed their API.)

But it is still fairly easy. (And so easy a virtual assistant or disgruntled teenager can do it.)

Twitter AutoPilot Tool No. 3: SnapBird

I told you these names were ridiculous.

But as silly as SnapBird sounds, it's actually a pretty cool tool. Because SnapBird lets you find people based on keywords.

And way more powerful than the generic Twitter search.

Now like all these tools, there is a FREE and PAID version. (For unlimited search requests you gotta pay.)

But here are a couple of great ways to use SnapBird:

- Search for users who have engaged with you
- Comb through old tweets of yours you

can't find

- Find the EXACT kind of lead you're looking for (Not just a generic group of might-be-leads)

Twitter AutoPilot Tool No. 4: Other Cool/Crazy Tools

There are some other neat tools I like, but don't use day in and day out.

Clicktotweet is a simple way to promote your stuff by letting people click a button which automatically updates their Tweet status with a pre-populated tweet promoting your Twitter goodness.

Twtqpon.com is probably the best of the bunch, as it allows you to create an online coupon code that your readers can redeem. It's a very cool way to spread the word (and the profits.)

And I'm sure by the time I finish typing this sentence, 1200 more Twitter tools will come out that can help you market to the masses.

Just try a couple out and see if they can help you. Chances are there's a fourteen-year-old RIGHT NOW inventing something in his basement that will help you make money in the future.

Chapter 10 Key Takeaways:

- **Try out tools like HootSuite or SocialOomph to manage ALL of your social media activity.** (And schedule your tweets weeks in advance — so you don't lose your frickin' mind.)

- **Rely on the ever-reliable Friend or Follow to help you build up your Twitter rapidly.** (By helping you get rid of the Twitter unfollower deadweight.

- **Use SnapBird to find users** who match your ideal customer interests and locations.

- **Explore crazy tools like ClicktoTweet and Twtqpon** to find that tool that'll make your Twitter marketing life much easier.

Epilogue: This Wasn't Supposed to Happen

Twitter, like most technological innovations, was a total accident. (And was never intended to be anything but a side project for the guys working on it.)

It started off as a simple micro-messaging service that helped colleagues keep in contact during the workday. (The reason for the 140-character limit was based on SMS cell phone limits and had little to do with the relative merits of a super-short tweet length.)

And yet, Ev Williams and Biz Stone, the founders of Twitter, certainly couldn't have predicted they would create a technology platform that would change the way we write, read, communicate and live.

But they did.

And today, Twitter is used just as much by bored suburban teenagers who want to be vampires as it is by student protesters in the Arab world dreaming of a new life.

And that's the mind-boggling part of Twitter.

Messages can spread in a matter of seconds to thousands of people you'll never meet.

And unlike platforms such as Facebook or LinkedIn, Twitter isn't about getting membership into an exclusive club or building your "network of friends."

It's about breaking down the doors of the club and finding out if your message resonates with the world.

Now, it's possible you won't be sending out tweets that bring down a fascist regime.

But...

Every once in a while you will send out

something that spreads like wildfire. (I sent out a bittersweet tweet about my mom's chemotherapy struggles that got 1,300 retweets and some of the most moving and heart-felt emails ever.)

So, as you plan your Twitter marketing calendar, just remember beyond the tech and the jargon and the ninja-hack strategies…

…in business we like to buy stuff from people we like and trust.

And people who remind us, in a simple way, how important it is to stay upbeat, strong and committed to what we want don't come off as marketers.

They appear as people, just like us.

Here's hoping the tips in this book help you not only become the trustworthy and likable Twitter ninja I know you can be…

…but bring a little "us-ness" to the world.

Good luck with your Twitter marketing, and if you'd like to drop me a line to tell me what you thought of this book, you can email me at michael@punkrockmarketing.com.

And if you've enjoyed this book, or even if you didn't enjoy the book, would you be willing to leave a review?

Even a sentence or two really helps us indie authors carve out a career as a creative professional.

Head over to PunkRockMarketing.com/TBook to leave a review on Amazon (and enjoy truckloads of good karma):

Oh, and just one more thing…

A Special FREE Gift for You!

If you'd like FREE instant access to my seminar "How to Make a Damn Good Living With Social Media (Even If You Hate Social Media" then head over to **PunkRockMarketing.com/Free**. (What else you gonna do? Watch another "Twilight" movie?!)

DISCLAIMER AND/OR LEGAL NOTICES:

Every effort has been made to accurately represent this book and it's potential. Results vary with every individual, and your results may or may not be different from those depicted. No promises, guarantees or warranties, whether stated or implied, have been made that you will produce any specific result from this book. Your efforts are individual and unique, and may vary from those shown. Your success depends on your efforts, background and motivation.

The material in this publication is provided for educational and informational purposes only and is not intended as business advice. Use of the programs, advice, and information contained in this book is at the sole choice and risk of the reader.

Printed in Great Britain
by Amazon